UNDERSTANDING BAPTISM

What Does it Mean?

Janine McNally

UNDERSTANDING BAPTISM
What Does it Mean?

Janine McNally
Equipping Fireflies, Inc.

Panama City, FL 34957
Janine@EquippingFireflies.com

Dear Parents

Your child is taking a significant step by indicating an interest in baptism. As they read this book, they will learn about knowing God, how to grow to become more like Him, and what baptism means. You have the privilege to be a part of this discipleship process by encouraging them and stepping in to help when needed.

Remember:
- Pray for your child that they will grow to know Jesus more each day.
- Don't expect your children to be perfect. Even though they may be saved, they are still sinners.

The depth to which your child will apply these lessons depends largely on your encouragement as a parent. Help them look up bible verses and write answers in their books.

Make the most of this opportunity, and you will see its fruit for years!

We are praying for you!

> "These commandments that I give you today are to be on your hearts. Impress them on your children. Talk about them when you sit at home, when you walk along the road when you lie down, and when you get up."
> Deuteronomy 6:6-7 [NIV].

UNDERSTANDING BAPTISM

What Does It Mean?

SALVATION: HOW TO KNOW JESUS

The first thing we will discuss is how to know for sure that you are going to heaven one day.

Do you ever wonder what will happen after you die?
Is it possible to know for sure that you are going to heaven?

The Bible says we can be saved by BELIEVING that Jesus paid our sin penalty IN FULL.

But first, there is some BAD news. We have a problem.

The BAD NEWS

1. We Have All Sinned.

Our big problem is that heaven is PERFECT, and we are NOT! If we went to heaven, we would ruin it because we are sinners.

Read this Bible verse:

> *"For all have sinned and fall short of the glory of God."*
> Romans 3:23.

What is sin? _____

_____

Write down some examples of sin. _____

_____

Sin is anything that breaks God's perfect standard.

Have you ever told a lie? _____

Have you ever stolen something? _____

Have you ever been mean to your brother or sister? _____

Have you ever disobeyed your parent or teacher? _____

Perhaps you didn't answer every question with a "yes," but even if you have done only one thing wrong, it means you're a "sinner."

Every one of us has sinned.

Because we have sinned, we have "*fallen short*" of "*God's glory.*" God's "glory" is His perfection. He is perfect, pure, and without sin.

His standard is 100% perfect. Not 99% or 98%, and He cannot be in the presence of sin.

If someone asked you to throw a rock from here to the North Pole, how far do you think you could throw? _____

_____

You might be able to throw further than someone else, but there is no way that you would reach the goal.
You would fall short.

God's "glory" is perfection. He is sinless. He is perfect. We have all fallen short of His standard.

Just one sin ruins perfection.

Imagine a hot summer, and someone offers you a glass of cool, fresh spring water. But just before they give you the glass, they drop a tiny droplet of deadly poison into the drink.

Why wouldn't you drink it? _____

Just one drop of poison ruined the pure water. And just one sin makes us sinners.

And that sin separates us from God.

Some of us might live "better lives" than others, but none can reach God's perfect standard. Heaven is perfect. No sin is allowed there.

2. Sin Results in Death.

This is more bad news! The Bible says,

> "For the WAGES of sin is death, but the gift of God is
> eternal life, through Jesus Christ our Lord."
> Romans 6:23.

Imagine if you worked for me for a day, and I paid you $50. That $50 is your "wage." That's what you earned.

The Bible says that our sin has earned "death." The penalty for sin is death.

We are separated from God forever because of our sins.

That's really bad news!

Thankfully, there is some... Good News!

The GOOD NEWS

1. Jesus Died for Us.

The Bible says:

> "But God demonstrates His own love for us in this:
> While we were still sinners, Christ died for us."
> Romans 5:8.

What did Jesus Christ do for us? _____

_____

Suppose you're in a hospital dying of cancer.

If I could take the cancer from your body and put it into mine,
what would happen to you? _____

_____

What would happen to me? _____

_____

The Bible says that Jesus took the punishment for our sins, and He died in our place. He took the sin from our "body" and put it onto His. He took the punishment we deserved. He paid the sin penalty for us.

Isn't that amazing?

After that, He came back to life, proving that sin was beaten. That's good news, but there is even more GOOD NEWS!

God took our sins upon Himself.

When Christ died for our sins, He took our punishment for us.

Read the next verse.

Underline what Jesus did for us.

Draw a GREEN circle around what happens to us.

> *"He himself bore our sins in His body on the cross... by His wounds, you have been healed."*
> 1 Peter 2:24.

How did Jesus die? _____

_____

Jesus shed His blood for us, and His blood cleanses us.

Read the following two verses and draw a RED circle around the word "blood."

> "The blood of Jesus, His Son, purifies us from all sin."
> 1 John 1:7.

> "Without the shedding of blood, there is no forgiveness."
> Hebrews 9:22.

In the times of the Old Testament, God commanded that the Israelites offer animal sacrifices as a means of seeking forgiveness.

But when Jesus came, that wasn't needed anymore.

> "He sacrificed for their sins once for all when He offered himself"
> Hebrews 7:27.

Why do you think it wasn't necessary to offer animal sacrifices any longer?

How many times did Jesus sacrifice for our sins? _____

_____

Animal sacrifices are no longer needed because Jesus paid the full penalty, once and for all!

> *"But if we walk in the light, as He is in the light, we have fellowship with one another, and the blood of Jesus, His Son, purifies us from all sin."*
> 1 John 1:7.

What does Jesus' blood do for us? _____

_____

After Jesus died, He was buried in a grave.
Three days later, something amazing happened. Jesus came back to life, proving that sin and death were defeated.

Jesus' death has cleansed us from our sins. Read this verse, and put a RED circle around the "color" words.

> "Come now, let us settle the matter," says the Lord. "Though your sins are like scarlet, they shall be as white as snow."
> Isaiah 1:18

What color were our sins? _____

What color are they now? _____

That's good news, but there is even more GOOD NEWS!

2. Do You Believe This?

The Bible says:

> "For God so loved the world that He gave His only Son,
> that whoever BELIEVES in Him will not perish,
> but have eternal life."
> John 3:16.

Draw a GREEN circle around what God has done for us.
Draw a BLUE circle around what our response should be.
Draw a RED circle around what we get when we believe.

What does it mean to believe? _____

_____

When you sit in a chair, do you inspect the legs first? _____

Do you check that the back of the chair is firmly attached?

_____

I trust that the chair will hold me up when I sit down. Believing in Jesus is the same as trusting Him.

We are sinners, and the penalty for sin is death. Jesus says that He died in our place.

He promises that whoever BELIEVES in Him has eternal life.

If His death paid the penalty, we are saved.
Do you believe that Jesus paid for your sins? (Circle one).

Yes   No   Not Sure

If Jesus paid for all of our sins, there is nothing more that is needed. We might think that our good works help.

What are some good works that people do? _____

_____

_____

The Bible says:

> "How, then, can we be saved? All of us have become like one who is unclean, and all our righteous acts are like filthy rags."
> Isaiah 64:5-6

What does God think of our good works? _____

_____

Do you get gifts at Christmas or on your birthday?

Imagine if a friend gave you a special gift.
How would you feel if, after you open it, they asked you to pay for it? Would it be a gift if you had to pay for it? _____

Imagine another situation.
When your friend gives you a gift, you offer to pay them for it instead of taking it.

How do you think they would feel? _____

_____

Heaven is a gift.

It doesn't cost you anything (Jesus paid the price!).
Nor can you pay for it. If you could, Jesus wouldn't have had to
die!

It is impossible to earn our way to heaven.
Nothing you DO can get you to heaven.
Jesus did it ALL!

Jesus paid the penalty for ALL our sins, past, present, and
future.

The Bible says:

> *"Very truly, I tell you, whoever hears my word and
> believes Him who sent Me has eternal life and will not
> be judged but has crossed over from death to life."*
> John 5:24.

What does God promise those who hear and believe Him?

That is the BEST gift ever!

Thought Questions

Have you trusted in Jesus alone to save you? (Circle One).

Yes	No	Not Sure

If you died tonight, are you sure where you would go? (Circle One).

Heaven	Not Sure

CAN YOU BE SURE?

Now that you have believed in Jesus, how can you be SURE that you are going to heaven when you die?

So many Christians believe in Jesus when they are young but then wonder:

"Did I do it right?" "Did it work?"
"But I just sinned really badly."

How can you be sure that you are saved?
Let's take a look at those questions, one at a time.

QUESTION #1. "Did I Do it Right?"

It's easy to fall into the trap of thinking,

>"I didn't do it right."
>"I didn't pray the right prayer."
>"I did something wrong."

What is wrong with thinking that way? _____

_____

How did you become a Christian? _____

Did you DO anything? _____

You might have prayed, filled out a card, or raised your hand, but those things don't save us! Only "believing" saves us!

Remember – WE don't DO anything because Jesus did it ALL.

Remember:

> "For God so loved the world that He gave His only Son,
> that whoever BELIEVES in Him will not perish,
> but have eternal life."
> John 3:16.

Remember what it means to believe? You could say it like this.

"Believing that Jesus died on the cross and paid the price for ALL of my sins, I am placing my trust in Him alone for the free gift of eternal life with Him in heaven."

Whenever you doubt your salvation, remember what the Bible says.

Jesus died for ALL your sins (past, present, and future).

The Bible says,

> *"Looking to Jesus, the founder and perfecter of our faith..."*
> Hebrews 12:2 ESV

Jesus is the One who made our faith possible. He is the One who paid the price for our sins.

It is only because of this that we can be saved.

So, when you doubt, look to Jesus! Look at the cross!

Remember what Jesus did for us!

QUESTION #2. "Did it work?"

Another mistake we make is wondering, "Did it work?" Did God really hear me? Does He really save us when we believe?

Answer these questions to see if you remember what we already talked about

Does God keep His promises? _____

What does He promise if we believe in Jesus? _____

_____

Remember what the Bible says:

> *"Whoever hears my Word*
> *and believes Him who sent Me HAS eternal life."*
> John 5:24.

Jesus said that if we believe, we HAVE eternal life. We can trust God's promise.

Just as we trusted Him for eternal life, we can trust Him to keep His promises for the rest of our lives.

Remember: When you doubt, look at the cross!

Jesus died so that we could spend eternity with Him. We can trust Him.

QUESTION #3.
"But I Just Sinned Really Badly?"

Unfortunately, we are all sinners. Becoming a Christian doesn't change that. Hopefully, as we grow, we will learn from our mistakes and become more like Jesus. But we will never be perfect until we get to heaven.

When you doubt and feel unsure, don't look at your life – it will never be perfect! Looking at your sin will make you doubt.

So, what should we do when we sin?

Confessing Our Sin.

Unfortunately, sin will always be a part of our life. Sin always separates us from God. But once we've believed in Jesus, what does sin do?

The Bible gives us the answer. Read this verse.

> *"If we confess our sins, He [God] is faithful and just and will forgive us our sins and purify us from all unrighteousness"*
> 1 John 1:9.

What does this verse tell us about God? _____

_____

What will God do if we confess our sins? _____

_____

"Confess" is a big word that means "to say the same thing." In other words, if we say the same thing as God, we are "confessing."

God says:	We agree:
"Stealing is wrong."	"Stealing is wrong."
"Telling lies is wrong."	"Telling lies is

When we say the same thing as God, we agree that "sin is wrong!" This is called "confession."

Once we confess our sins, God promises to forgive us. You might wonder what that means. How long does God's forgiveness last? What if we sin again?

Another word for "sin" is "transgression."
Read the verses below, and draw a BLUE circle around anything you think is special.

> "As far as the east is from the west, so far has He [God] removed our transgressions [sins] from us."
> Psalm 103:12.

How far is it from the east to the west? _____

_____

When God forgives us, He casts our sins far, far away. He forgives us completely, meaning He doesn't hold any of our sins against us once we confess them. They are gone. Forgiven!

> *"I, even I, am He who blots out your transgressions, for my own sake, and remembers your sins no more."*
> Isaiah 43:25.

> *"For I will forgive their wickedness and will remember their sins no more."*
> Jeremiah 31:34.

> *"Their sins and lawless acts I will remember no more."*
> Hebrews 8:12.

Does God keep a record of our sins? _____

God's forgiveness is complete – He doesn't hold a grudge or bring up our past sins later, saying, "Remember when you did that bad thing?"

How does it make you feel knowing God has forgiven you for
EVERYTHING? _____

_____

Experiment

Supplies Needed:
1. Ground black pepper
2. A plate
3. Water
4. Dish soap

Directions:
1. Pour some water onto the plate.
2. Sprinkle a bit of pepper all over the water.
3. Dip your finger into some dish soap and then into the pepper water.

What happened to the pepper when you put your finger into

the water? _____

_____

Our sins are forgiven when we confess them. But that doesn't mean that we don't need to learn and grow.

The Bible says:

> *"Therefore, if anyone is in Christ, the new creation has come: The old has gone, the new is here."*
> 2 Corinthians 5:17.

We are now a brand-new creation.

Are you thankful for what Jesus did for you? _____

Do you want to please Him? _____

We do that by becoming more like Him every day.

Thought Questions

Now that you believe in Jesus, you are a "Christian." God wants us to become more like Jesus.

What are some things that we can do to please God?

_____

_____

Look up the following verses and write the answer down. Have your parent or leader help you.

> *"All Scripture is God-breathed and is useful for teaching, rebuking, correcting and training in righteousness."*
> 2 Timothy 3:16

What will help us learn and grow?

_____

_____

> "Don't let anyone look down on you because you are young, but set an example for the believers in speech, in conduct, in love, in faith, and in purity."
> 1 Timothy 4:12.

How should we behave?

_____

_____

> "I have hidden your word in my heart that I might not sin against you."
> Psalm 119:11

What can we do to become more like Jesus (and sin less)?

_____

_____

There is one more thing that God says we should do.

Read this next verse. What does it say?

> "...not giving up meeting together, as some are in the habit of doing, but encouraging one another—and all the more as you see the Day approaching."
> Hebrews 10:25.

What is a good habit for us according to this verse?

_____

_____

We need each other. It's important to make it a habit to attend church and learn from others.

The best thing you can do is find someone older than you (besides your parent) and ask them to help you. Find someone that you know loves Jesus; maybe a Sunday School teacher or a friend from church.

Can you think of anyone who might be able to help you?

_____

Spend time with them and talk to them about your life.

Now that you are sure you are saved, we will talk about the first thing God wants us to do.

WHAT IS BAPTISM?

Once we have trusted in Jesus as our Savior, the very first thing that God asks us to do is to be baptized. He wants us to tell others, and one way to show that we love Jesus is to be baptized.

The Bible says:

> "Therefore, go and make disciples of all nations, baptizing them in the name of the Father and of the Son and of the Holy Spirit."
> Matthew 28:19.

The first command is to "make disciples."

What is the second command? _____

Once we have trusted in Jesus as our Savior, the very first thing that God asks us to do is to be baptized. He wants us to tell others.

Several stories in the Bible teach us about baptism.

Read these verses in Acts. They tell the story of a man named Philip. He meets another man while he's traveling.

He begins to tell him about Jesus. Underline anything that you think is important.

> *"Then Philip began with that very passage of Scripture and told him the good news about Jesus.*
> *As they traveled along the road, they came to some water, and the eunuch said,*
> *"Look, here is water. What can stand in the way of my being baptized?"*
> *And he gave orders to stop the chariot.*
> *Then, both Philip and the eunuch went down into the water, and Philip baptized him."*
> Acts 8:35-38.

NOTE: A "eunuch" is another name for a "servant."

Phillip was teaching the eunuch the "good news" about Jesus from the Old Testament.

What "good news" do you think he was teaching?

_____

After hearing about Jesus, the servant believed and was immediately baptized.

Here is another story.

Peter was preaching to a crowd of people about Jesus being put to death on the cross and coming back to life three days later.

This is what happened when they heard his message.

> *"Those who accepted his message were baptized, and about three thousand were added to their number that day."*
> Acts 2:41.

What do you think it means when it says they "accepted his

message?" _____

_____

How many were baptized? _____

When were they baptized? _____

Here is another example. It's another story about Philip.

This time, he was preaching to a group of people.

> *"But when they believed Philip as he preached the good news of the kingdom of God and the name of Jesus Christ, they were baptized, both men and women."*
> Acts 8:12.

The Bible has many stories like this.
People believed in Jesus and were baptized.

What did they do after hearing the good news? _____

_____

The Bible is clear about our need to be baptized after we believe in Jesus. But what does baptism mean?

What is the Meaning of BAPTISM?

1. Baptism is a Picture

Baptism is a picture of Jesus' burial and resurrection.

When you are baptized, you will be lowered under the water and then brought back up again.

Going down into the water is a picture of Jesus' death and burial.

> "We were therefore **buried** with him through baptism into death..."
> Romans 6:4.

Coming up out of the water is a picture of Jesus rising from the dead.

> "...just as Christ was **raised** from the dead through the glory of the Father, we too may live a new life."
> Romans 6:4

Read the next verse.
Draw a PURPLE circle around the words that describe the meaning of Baptism.

> "Having been buried with Him in baptism, in which you were also raised with Him through your faith in the working of God, who raised Him from the dead."
> Colossians 2:12

So, baptism is a picture of Jesus being buried under [in] the ground and then being raised up to life.

A Brand New Life

When we first believed in Jesus, we became a brand new person with a brand new life.

> *"Therefore, if anyone is in Christ, he is a new creation; the old has gone, the new has come!"*
> 2 Corinthians 5:17

What do we become when we believe in Jesus Christ?

_____

When you are lifted out of the water, it is a picture of being raised up to a brand new life, a life with Jesus.

A Brand New Family

Baptism also connects us to other Christians. The Bible describes the church as the "body of Christ" – God's people on the earth.

When we are baptized, there is a real sense of being joined together with other believers.

> *"For we were all baptized by one Spirit into **one body**."*
> 1 Corinthians 12:12-13

What does the verse say that we are baptized into?

_____

Being baptized shows that we are a part of God's family.

We became part of God's family when we first believed. We SHOW that we are a part of God's family when we are baptized.

2. Baptism is a Symbol

A Wedding Ring

When a couple gets married, they usually exchange rings.

What do you think is the reason for wearing a wedding ring?

_____

If I put a wedding ring on your finger, does that mean you are

married? _____

A wedding ring doesn't make you married. It simply shows people that you are married and love the person you are married to.

Getting baptized doesn't make you a follower of Jesus. That happened when you first believed in Jesus. Baptism is simply a way to show people on the outside what has happened to you on the inside. It's a symbol of your love for Jesus.

A Sport's Team Jersey

Do you like watching football or basketball?
Or perhaps you play soccer or baseball.

Why do people wear a sports jersey with their team's name on it

during a game? _____

_____

Getting baptized is like putting on a sports team jersey.

You are saying to everyone that you are on Jesus' team. You belong to Him.

If you have trusted in Jesus to save you, you are on His team forever and will want everyone to know it.

Why Should I Be Baptized?

1. Being Baptized Obeys God's Command.

Baptism is the first thing God commands us to do once we have believed.

Draw a RED circle around the things we are commanded to do.

> *"Therefore, go and make disciples of all nations,*
> *baptizing them in the name of the Father and of the Son and*
> *of the Holy Spirit,*
> *and teaching them to obey everything I have commanded you.*
> *And surely, I am with you always, to the very end of the age."*
> Matthew 28:19-20

God wants us to "Go" and "make disciples" of everyone, everywhere.

Making disciples is another way of saying, "Tell others about Jesus and help them believe the good news."

Water baptism is an act of faith and obedience to God's command.

2. Being Baptized Pleases God.

Did you know that Jesus was baptized?

He was not a sinner, yet he obeyed the command to be baptized.

He wanted to set an example for us to follow.

> *"At that time, Jesus came from Nazareth in Galilee and was baptized by John in the Jordan."*
> Mark 1:9.

The next two verses tell us how God felt about His Son, Jesus, being baptized.

Draw an ORANGE circle around the words describing how God felt about His Son, Jesus, being baptized.

"Just as Jesus was coming up out of the water, He saw heaven being torn open and the Spirit descending on Him like a dove. And a voice came from heaven:
"You are My Son, whom I love; with You, I am well pleased."
Mark 1:10-11.

How did God feel about Jesus being baptized? _____

_____

3. Being Baptized is a Public Declaration

When people hear that you want to be baptized, it tells them that something significant has happened in your life, and you want them to know about it.

Baptism lets people know that you are a follower of Jesus Christ. It is a public confession of your faith in Him and shows you are committed to Him.

People can't SEE when you believe.

You might believe in Jesus at church, at home, in your bedroom, or anywhere.

If you don't tell someone, they won't know.

The most important thing to understand is that baptism doesn't save you. Rather, it shows others that you have believed in Jesus and are ALREADY saved.

Are you on "Team Jesus"? _____

What Does "BAPTISM" Mean?

The word "baptize" comes from a Greek word which means "to immerse or dip under water."

> "As soon as Jesus was baptized,
> He went up out of the water."
> Matthew 3:16

Have you seen a baptism before? What happened?

_____

_____

_____

Baptisms are different from church to church.

Most churches baptize people by "immersion." That means you will go under the water.

The pastor (or perhaps someone else) will ask if you have trusted Jesus as your Savior.

What will your answer be? _____

Then, you will walk together down into the water.

You will hold your breath, and the leader will briefly lower you under the water.

The leader will then lift you back up out of the water.

Am I Ready to Be Baptized?

How do you know if you are ready to be baptized?

The Bible teaches us that we should be baptized after we believe in Jesus.

Answer the following questions.

1. Are you ready to be baptized? _____

2. Have you believed in Jesus alone? _____

3. Are you sure that you are saved? _____

If your answers are "yes," then, yes! You are ready.

Talk with your parents and your leader about it this week.

Memory Verse Activity

Use the keypad to decode the verse and write it out below.

"367 48 47 29 GRACE 968 4283

2336 saved, through faith 263

8447 47 6683766 yourselves;

48 47 843 gift 63 God."

Ephesians 2:8 (NIV).

"_____ ____ ____ _____ GRACE _____ _____

_____ saved, through faith - _____ _____ ____

_____ ____ yourselves;

____ ____ _____ gift ____ God."

Ephesians 2:8 (NIV).

Try to learn this verse this week.

It's a great reminder that salvation is a FREE gift!

"MY STORY"

Write your salvation story (your "testimony") this week on the next pages. Answer these questions:

1. How did you become a Christian?

_____

_____

_____

_____

_____

_____

_____

_____

2. When and where were you?

_____

_____

_____

_____

_____

_____

_____

_____

_____

_____

_____

3. How has becoming a Christian changed you?

_____

_____

_____

_____

_____

_____

_____

_____

_____

_____

Congratulations!

You have now completed "Understanding Baptism." Fill in your Certificate of Completion with your name and the date. Ask your parent or leader to sign it for you.

Certificate of Completion
Awarded to

_____

On _____ _____ _____
       Month   Day   Year

For completing UNDERSTANDING BAPTISM

Presented by _____
                          Signature

Other resources available from Equipping Fireflies.

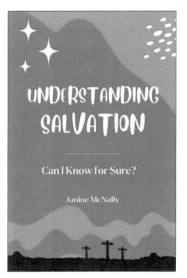

UNDERSTANDING SALVATION is designed for children ages 7-12 to use independently or with a parent.

It presents the good news of Jesus in a clear and easy-to-understand way that will help them know FOR SURE that they will live with Jesus in heaven one day.

Children will learn the key principles of salvation, teaching the "Bad News" (sin) and "Good News" (Jesus), along with Bible verses and simple illustrations. This 60-page book will help them deepen their understanding of God's grace and begin their relationship with Him.

UNDERSTANDING the BIBLE is the third book in the "Understanding Life" series for kids.

When your child asks the tough questions, do you have answers for them?

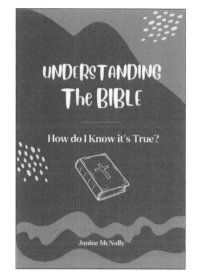

- How do we know the Bible is true?
- Is the Bible trustworthy?
- How do we know that it is really God's Word?

Written for children ages 8-12, this 70-page book teaches some basic Bible apologetics. The content covers:

Three Big Words:
1. Inspiration - Written by God and Man
2. Inerrancy - No mistakes
3. Preservation

The Bible's Structure

How to Have a Quiet Time

How to Memorize God's Word

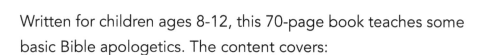

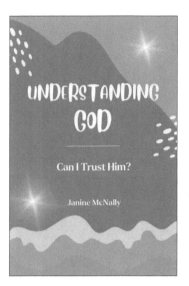

UNDERSTANDING GOD

Can I Trust Him?

Janine McNally

UNDERSTANDING GOD is the fourth in the "Understanding Life" books for Kids. Children are asking questions every day about God, the Bible, salvation, life, death, the afterlife, angels, demons, and more.

We need to be prepared with answers, or they will look elsewhere.

This 94-page book answers the following questions.

1. What is God like?
2. How did He create the World?
3. Who Created God?
4. Who is the Holy Spirit?
5. How can Jesus be God but also be God's Son?
6. Why does God let bad things happen?
7. Can God make mistakes?
8. Does God Love Me?

This book can be used as a training resource for your volunteers or as a parent.

UNDERSTANDING ME addresses the big question, "Who am I?" in this 85-page book for kids ages 9-12.

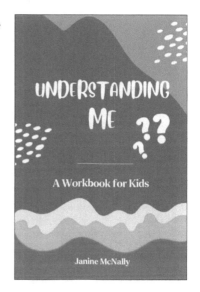

Our world says, "There's no right or wrong," "We decide what is true and right," and "We can create our own identity." At a time when kids are going through enormous changes, they are confronted with ambiguity and confusion.

1. Who am I?
2. Am I loved?
3. Am I alone?
4. Why am I here?

Each question is handled from a Biblical perspective and ends with the hope of a new life, a new body, and a new world for those who have trusted in Jesus.

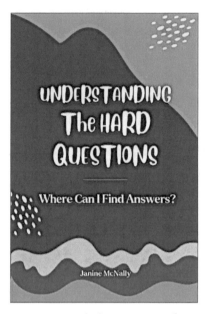

UNDERSTANDING HARD QUESTIONS is the sixth book in the "Understanding Life" series for kids. It answers 56 of the most common questions asked by kids from a Biblical perspective and in an age-appropriate way.

- Who created God?
- Does God speak to people?
- Will God stop loving me if I keep sinning?
- How did Jesus perform miracles?
- Why do people get sick and die?
- Why did my parents get divorced?
- Can Christians lose their salvation?
- How can God forgive murderers?
- Why is sex outside of marriage wrong?
- Are there more than two genders?
- Can I be sure that I will go to heaven?

Written for kids ages 9-12, this 128-page book teaches basic Bible apologetics.

UNDERSTANDING LIFE & DEATH is written for children ages 8-12 and addresses the questions that arise when a child experiences the death of a loved one.

- Why Do People Get Sick and Die?
- What Happens After You Die?
- If God Loves Me, Why Did My Dad Die?
- What is Heaven Like?
- Will Everyone Go to Heaven No Matter What They Believe?
- Do People Who Never Hear About Jesus Go to Heaven?
- Is Hell Real?
- How Could a Loving God Send People to Hell?
- Why Did God Create Satan?

These questions and more in this 104-page are answered from a Biblical perspective in an age-appropriate way with the goal of providing help and hope in a time of sadness and grief.

Made in United States
Troutdale, OR
06/16/2024

20607278R00040